# YOUNG
# IN THE
# TWENTIES

Eleanor Allen

A & C Black · London

Allen, Eleanor,
    Young in the Twenties.
    1. Great Britain—Social life and
    customs—20th century—Juvenile
    literature
    I. Title
    941.083    DA566.4
    ISBN 0–7136–2854–5

Published by A & C Black (Publishers) Limited
35 Bedford Row, London WC1R 4JH

First published 1988

Filmset by August Filmsetting, Haydock, St Helens
Printed in Great Britain by The Bath Press

## Acknowledgements

My thanks are due to all the people who kindly talked to me
about the 1920s, filled in a questionnaire, or supplied
photographs or other background material. I am particularly
grateful to the following, whose personal recollections appear in
the book:

Mrs Barnes, Mr and Mrs F. Baker, Mr L. Bevan, Mrs L.
Bridges, Mr P. Clarke, Mr R. J. Collins, Mr and Mrs G.
Edenborough, Mr Evans, Mrs Jones, Mr R. Kearns, Mrs Elsie
Mills, Mrs Helen Pullen, Rachel Newbolt, Mrs K. Reynolds,
Mr J. Shearman, Mr and Mrs F. Smith, Mrs G. Stokes, Mrs
M. Watkins, Mrs S. Willis, Mrs G. Winter.


Pictures by Backnumbers 44(bottom right); Barnaby's Picture
Library 5(right), 8(bottom), 27, 28(bottom), 46(top); BBC
Hulton Picture Library 1, 4(bottom), 5(left), 6, 9, 12(bottom),
20(top), 21(left), 26(top), 28(top), 37(left top and bottom), 38,
39 (top), 43 (bottom), 45(top), 60, 61, 63; Beamish Open Air
Museum 6(bottom), 7(top), 8(top), 14, 15(top), 16, 22, 23(left),
24(top), 25, 29(top), 30(bottom), 32, 33, 34, 43(top), 49(top),
56(bottom), 58; Cinema Theatre Association Archive 42,
41(bottom); Mr R J Collins 52(bottom); The Co-op 19,
20(bottom), 48(bottom), 53(top); John Frost Historical
Newspaper Service 10(bottom), 12, 35, 36(bottom), 46(bottom),
59(right); Greater London Photograph Library 29(bottom), 59
(left); Illustrated London News Picture Library 4 (top),
15(bottom), 18(bottom), 41(top), 44(top), 54(middle and
bottom), 55(left), 57(top), 62(bottom); Dr M Knowles 52(top);
the London Transport Museum 11(bottom), 50(bottom),
51(top); London Borough of Hackney, Archives dept 48(top);
Mary Evans Picture Library 17(bottom), 23(right), 36(top), 37
(right), 39(bottom), 40, 45(bottom), 47, 50(top), 51(bottom),
54(top); Mrs D McLellan 31(top), 53(bottom), 55(right);
Museum of London 13, 17(top), 21(right); National Motor
Museum 7(bottom); National Museum of Labour History
10(top), 11(top); G H Soole Collection/NRM York 49(bottom);
J.Sainsbury's 18(top); Walter Skinner 26(bottom).

Before I could start writing this book I had
to get in touch with a lot of people who could
remember the 1920s. Some were friends,
neighbours or relatives of mine, others were
their friends or relatives. Many were people I
contacted through groups or clubs. I talked
to them, made notes or recordings of what
they said, or I asked them to fill in
questionnaires.

If you would like to find out more about
life in the 1920s yourself, you could try
asking people, as I did. On the whole they
will enjoy telling you about the past. But
don't forget that not everybody's memory is
always accurate (no matter how good it is).
Don't accept any fact someone tells you
unless you can find other people who will
back it up. And remember that the way
people lived differed a lot, depending on how
well-off they were, or which part of the
country they came from. Try to talk to
people from as many different backgrounds
as you can.

Eleanor Allen

# Contents

# Introduction

'Life was very different then... So different, I can hardly find the words to describe it...'

The beginning of the 1920s was very special to the people of Britain. They had just fought the First World War. For four years they had endured all the sadness, suffering and deprivation that war brings, until finally a truce was signed in November 1918. Now they pinned their hopes on the Twenties.

What would the decade bring? They hoped it would be full of gaiety to wipe out some of their harsher memories and, more important, that it would bring them some rewards.

Many people nowadays think of the Twenties as a gay, frivolous era. But underneath, it was a time of dissatisfaction, suspicion and depression, because a lot of people knew they were not getting the rewards they had hoped for.

▲ Armistice Day 1918. War ended at 11 am on 11 November. As the news spread, people took to the streets to cheer

▼ Poverty forced many families to live in slums

4

‘ We knew what we were missing – we could see around us people who could get the things we couldn't. We were very much aware of being poor. We were happy enough because we lived in a world of 'haves' and 'have-nots' and could not (short of a miracle) aspire to having things other people took for granted. But there was some bitterness . . . ’

‘ When we were growing up, we were very strongly aware of being 'haves' or 'have-nots'. It affected your whole way of life: what you ate, how you dressed, what jobs you could aim for — even your chances of a healthy life . . . Just about everything, in fact . . . ’

The 'haves' were the well-to-do upper and middle classes. They had managed to cling to many of the privileges and high living standards they had enjoyed before the War.

Upstairs, downstairs – guests arrive ▶ while the servants put the champagne on ice

▼ Guests at a ball to raise money for charity. The upper classes still enjoyed the privileges they had known before the war

The 'have-nots' were most of the working classes. They hoped the Twenties would bring changes to improve their lives. A 'land fit for heroes' was what they had fought for and what the politicians had promised them. They looked forward to good, secure jobs, improved housing and living standards, and better opportunities for their children.

Unfortunately, the 1920s failed to bring the majority of working class people any of those things.

# Unemployment

When the soldiers returned from the trenches, many wondered what they had been fighting for. There were few jobs and, for hundreds of thousands of people, the Twenties was a time of having to make ends meet on unemployment benefit.

Before the War, there had been a world-wide demand for British goods. Everybody was optimistic that, with peace, the demand would soon return. That didn't happen. For a couple of years there was a post-war boom, but by 1920 a sudden slump had set in. Nobody was keen to buy British any more. Whilst Britain had been concentrating all her efforts on fighting the War, other countries had been modernising and extending their industries. The old British industries such as cotton, coal mining, shipbuilding and iron and steel were behind the times.

Their methods and machines were slow and they couldn't compete. With world orders for these goods going elsewhere, production dropped, and as a result vast numbers of workers had to be laid off.

When employers did begin to modernise, the situation got worse, not better, because the new machines needed fewer workers to operate them.

▼ To help feed the unemployed, charitable organizations set up soup kitchens. Over two million men came home from the War to look for jobs, and many could not find work or a place to live

The slump in trade brought slack times and redundancies, especially for workers in the older, out of date industries. People in the North of England, Scotland and Wales suffered most, because that was where the old industries were mainly situated.

A busy iron foundry in 1919. By 1929 ▶ the number employed in the iron and steel industries had fallen by a fifth from pre-war totals

▼ The bull-nose Morris, being assembled on a production line at Cowley, 1925. By the late Twenties, methods of mass production had brought the price of a small car within the reach of middle class families

Working people who lived in the South of England and the Midlands did not suffer so much. There, new industries making products such as cars and chemicals had started to develop. These industries provided jobs with good wages. As a result, a great gap in living standards arose between the North and South. More 'haves' and 'have-nots' were produced: workers who had a job and wages to spend, and those who had no job, no prospects and no wages.

By June 1921 more than two million men were unemployed. Many remained out of work for most of the decade. Men were expected to be the 'breadwinners' for their families. Losing their jobs was a terrible blow to their self-respect. They had to live on unemployment benefit, known as the 'dole'. Dole money was very stingy. It barely covered the cost of food and rent, and left nothing for other essentials like heat and clothing. The payment was usually 15 shillings (75p) a week for a man and his wife, and just under 5s (25p) a week for each child. Some authorities would not pay out more than 40 or 50 shillings maximum, even if a family had more than a dozen children, because that was as much as a man could earn in a badly paid job. It was assumed that if men were paid more for not working, they wouldn't bother to look for a job.

▲ A village bread oven, where people who couldn't afford to heat their own oven could take their bread to be baked, or the Sunday lunch to be cooked

▼ Queueing for the 'dole'. Dole money was only intended to help people for a short while between jobs. After a few weeks, you had to apply to your local council for money

▲ A nun visits badly nourished women and children in the East End slums, 1926

People who had to exist on the dole, or on part-time work, remember the Twenties as a time of constantly 'making do', 'making ends meet' and 'getting by'. For them, it was a very bleak time indeed.

In 1920, a professor at London University worked out this minimum weekly budget for a docker, his wife and three children:

| | | |
|---|---|---|
| Food | £2.0s.0d | (£2.00) |
| Rent | £0.6s.6d | (33p) |
| Clothing | £0.12s.6d | (63p) |
| Fuel | £0.4s.8d | (24p) |
| **Sundries:** | | |
| Household | £0.3s.4d | (17p) |
| Personal | £0.6s.6d | (33p) |
| Total | £3.13s.6d | (£3.68) |

This budget allowed a generous £2 a week for food. But even then the food only included eight pints of milk, no butter – only margarine, no eggs and very little fruit and vegetables.

Experts, appointed by the Government, collected evidence to try and show how little per head a balanced diet could cost. But they didn't take into account the fact that a mother, living in squalid surroundings with ten children to feed, couldn't be expected to spend every day concocting ingenious economy meals. If she had the money, she was quite likely to blow it on the easy solution of a comforting portion of chips all round.

# Strikes

The Twenties was a period of industrial unrest as well as unemployment.

Even people who managed to keep their jobs in the old industries soon had plenty to feel unhappy about. They had hoped for increased productivity and higher wages, leading to a better standard of living for themselves and their families. Instead, they found that they were being forced to accept even lower wages than they had been paid before the War. This led to strikes throughout the 1920s.

In 1926 there was a general strike and the whole country was brought to a standstill: no public transport, no factories working, no newspapers. It came about because the coal miners, who were already very badly paid for working long hours in terrible conditions, were told by the mine owners that, in order to make coal cheaper to sell abroad, they would have to work even longer hours for even less pay. That was too much!

▲ This bus was destroyed for carrying 'blacklegs' – people who continued to work when their colleagues were on strike

'Not a penny off the pay, not a minute on the day' became the miners' slogan. On this occasion they were supported by the other trade unions.

On the morning of Tuesday, 5th May, Britain awoke to a general strike. The Government was ready. Troops were called in to keep the essential services going and many middle and upper class people volunteered their services. They had very little understanding of the workers' plight. Some saw the strike as a serious revolutionary threat, others saw it as a good chance for a 'lark'.

◀ A news bulletin the day after the General Strike began

The job of driving buses was a particularly dangerous one for volunteers. Buses were special targets for strikers armed with bricks and bottles. The job was frequently undertaken by students, who treated the situation with typical student humour. One bus is said to have carried a notice stating,

'The driver of this bus is a student of Guy's Hospital. The conductor of this bus is a student of Guy's. Anybody who interferes with either is liable to be a patient of Guy's.'

Even some of the working classes worked to break the strike.

❝ My father continued working to keep public transport running, even though he belonged to a trade union. My school mates seemed to think all strikers should be dealt with by the firing squad! Although I came from a working class background, I never bothered to consider that the strikers might have some right on their side. Had it taken place later, when I myself had left school and was trying to get a job, I might have viewed the strike differently. ❞

▲ 'Special constables' collecting their armbands and batons. They were mainly business or professional men and their job was to help volunteers through strikers' picket lines and demonstrations

▼ London buses, protected by armed troops

After only nine days, support for the miners began to collapse. They were left to carry on the strike alone. But without the support of the other unions, they couldn't win. They struggled on with the strike for seven months, and their families suffered many hardships.

‘ The situation was so bad, food-wise, that one or two local butchers and tradesmen formed a committee to supply food to under-nourished children. It was a gesture of goodwill to past and future customers. ’

With the mines closed down, even miners' families were short of coal for their fires.

‘ I remember picking coal on disused slag heaps. By delving and scratching you could unearth pieces of coal. You put it in a bag and humped it home as best you could. I remember half a dozen miners at Newhill, where there was a coal outcrop, started their own mining operations and supplied neighbours with coal until the police stopped them. ’

In the end, the miners were forced to go back to work for even longer hours and even less pay. They had achieved nothing at all.

▼ Headlines from the Daily Express, 13 May 1926. The General Strike is called off, but the miners stay out on strike until 12 November

▲ During the strike, the shortage of coal affected everyone, including miners. These children are searching for bits of coal in dustboxes which contain ash swept from other people's fireplaces

# Homes

Nowadays many families own their own homes. But it was different in the early Twenties. In those days it was more usual to rent your house from a private landlord, even if you were well-off.

Unfortunately, the renting system wasn't working too well. Many landlords, especially those who rented run-down properties, didn't spend enough money on repairs. As a result, many families lived in houses that had been allowed to deteriorate badly over the years. There were cracked walls, rotting woodwork and leaking roofs. Tenants dared not complain because there was a great shortage of houses. They feared that if they complained they would be evicted and would end up with no roof over their heads at all.

In towns and cities, there was a further problem. The houses were often too small and cramped for the size of the families that lived in them, and they were tightly packed together in narrow, dark streets. Many had been built before the time of running water, indoor toilets and bathrooms. People living in these older houses often had to share one lavatory and tap with several other families – outside, across a yard.

▼ Many poor families lived in cramped and unsanitary conditions. There was no Social Security. Help from the Salvation Army was often the most they could hope for

Repair and improvement was not always the answer. In small houses there was no space to install the amenities that would bring them up to standard. Demolition and rebuilding was often the only solution. But slum clearance did not get under way on a large scale until the 1930s, so throughout the Twenties a large slice of the population had to endure squalid and unhealthy surroundings.

▲ These tightly packed houses were to be demolished in the slum clearance of the 1930s

▼ A miner taking his bath. The water would have been heated on a coal fire in the kitchen

❛ I was brought up in a miner's house – two up and two down. There was difficulty in housing a mixed family like ours. The four of us children had to share one bedroom – my brother and I in a double bed, and half the room partitioned off with a curtain for my sisters. We had to bathe in front of the kitchen fire in a galvanised tin bath which hung on a hook outside the door when not in use. In windy weather we had to get it in because it clanged against the wall and kept us awake. There was an outdoor lavatory at the end of the yard. Behind it was a midden. There was a fearsome smell and it was plagued with flies. In summer we had to use lots of red powder to kill them. ❜

There was a desperate need for new houses. But private landlords felt they could not make enough profit out of building houses for workers. To solve the problem, local councils took on the responsibility of building houses that could be rented out to better-paid workers at reasonable rents. The 'council house' system had arrived.

❝ My dad had a good job, so eventually we moved from our back-to-back house to a bigger and better council house with a nice kitchen and gas boiler – and a bathroom, which in those days was considered posh! ❞

▼ Houses built for employees of the Consett Iron Company in Northumberland

Constance St. Back View. 22.2.21.

Building large new estates of council houses didn't really get going until later in the Twenties. These estates tended to be situated on the outskirts of towns, which meant that tenants had further to travel to work. But that was a small inconvenience, compared with the thrill of having their own lavatory, a hot water supply, a small garden and a bathroom.

▲ A 'planned' housing estate in Eastbourne, showing well-spaced houses with gardens

# Middle class homes and servants

‘ Our house (in London) was as big as the one my flat's in now. It's occupied by four families. But our old house was occupied by one family and their domestics. What a thing it was! Because my parents weren't all that rich. They were all right, you know. But my mother at that time could hardly exist without two living-in servants and a girl who looked after the children. And a char to come in, and somebody to have a go at the garden. And that has almost entirely gone, hasn't it? Nobody lives like that now, except pop stars and millionaires. ’

Life wasn't entirely without housing problems for the middle and upper classes. Their properties were better maintained, but many were very big and inconveniently designed, with several floors, long corridors and flights of stairs. Most of the housework was still laboriously done by hand, so well-off households employed plenty of servants.

In the earlier part of the Twenties, getting servants wasn't too much of a problem. The number of servants employed by a household showed how well-off the family was. Children wanting to show off weren't above inventing a housemaid or two.

▲ Squeezing clothes through a mangle to wring out some of the water before they were hung up to dry

Throughout the Twenties, even those families who couldn't afford a servant usually employed a 'char' to do the heavy work.

‘ We had some help in the house, as my mother was a victim of tuberculosis. A charlady came each Monday to do the washing with the aid of the copper boiler, fuelled by coal, and a heavy old-fashioned mangle with wooden rollers to wring out some of the water – and crush the buttons on my father's shirts and pants! She spent another day 'cleaning through', as it was termed then. ’

▲ Wealthy families would employ several servants, including a nanny, cook, parlourmaid, butler, footman, gardener and groom

As the decade wore on, servants became increasingly hard to find. Girls preferred to find jobs in factories or shops because the work was better paid and left them more free time.

' I left school at fourteen and went to work in a factory making overalls, boiler-suits and railwaymen's jackets. It was eight till five and the pay was 7s.6d (38p) a week. I went for a job in service first, but they expected even longer hours for less wages. They expected too much! '

▲ Factory girls working lathes at a Reeves water-colour and paint-brush factory

▼ An advertisement for vacuum cleaners. Although sales increased in the 1920s, they remained rather a luxury until the 1940s and 50s

*Another servant in the house this Christmas*

A smaller, easier-to-run house was a tempting alternative to the problems of hiring servants. By offering a sum of money for every house that was built, the Government encouraged builders to erect houses for the middle classes and highest paid workers. Cheap mortgages enabled people to buy the new houses. The big houses left vacant could be divided up and let as smaller units.

Many of the new private houses had electric lighting instead of gas. Housewives began to think about purchasing some of the new labour-saving gadgets, like electric irons and vacuum cleaners.

Unfortunately, the houses built at this time were very dreary to look at. They stretched for mile after mile in 'ribbon developments' along the sides of main roads, because it was cheaper to build them there.

# Shopping

There were no self-service shops in the Twenties. All customers had to ask over the counter for what they wanted, and queue patiently while other customers were being served. In a grocer's shop it could take ages to be served, because not many foods were pre-packed. Items like biscuits, sugar and flour had to be weighed. Butter had to be sliced and patted into shape, then carefully wrapped. At some shops, if you wanted to buy flour, you had to take a pillow-case to carry it home in. Customers sometimes got impatient with all the waiting, but not as often as you might imagine. Shops were a place to meet and talk; people weren't in such a rush to do their shopping as they are nowadays.

❛ You could be a hell of a time waiting. Yes, you got impatient sometimes. But it was better then. It's all hustle and bustle now . . . ❜

❛ We didn't mind being kept waiting. Time didn't seem to matter so much in those days . . . And nowadays, at Sainsbury's, I can tell you, it's not much faster. True, you can pick the goods up faster, but often you still have to queue to pay at the check-out. ❜

▲ 'At your service' – staff at an early Sainsbury's in Croydon

▼ Goods in a grocer's shop. The large tins contained loose biscuits which had to be weighed and wrapped

If you wanted a whole week's groceries, there was no need to go to the shop for them or take them home yourself. You could write out an order, or telephone the shop. The grocer would not only send a delivery boy with the goods on his bike, he would often call to collect written orders in person. Other traders such as butchers and fishmongers would also deliver orders.

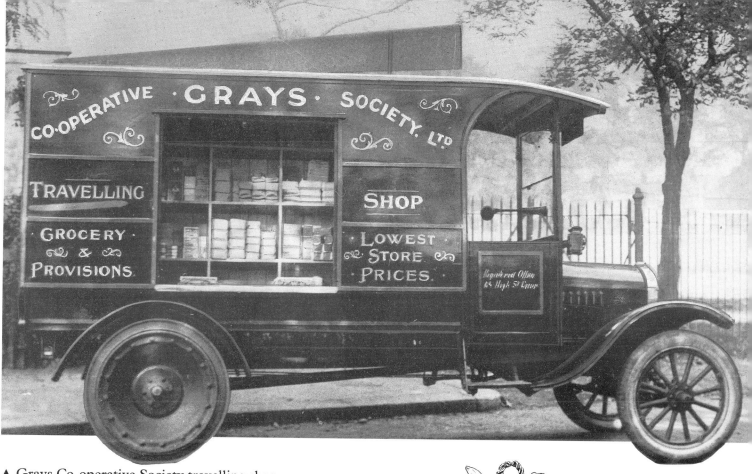

▲ Grays Co-operative Society travelling shop

▼ Milk churns and carts at a depot

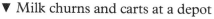

The baker, greengrocer, milkman and coalman all regularly brought their goods round on a cart to your door, and knocked to enquire what you would like. Milk didn't come in bottles in those days: it was sold from a big metal churn transported on a cart. The amount you wanted was measured into a metal cylinder, then poured into your own basin or jug. Poor families couldn't afford to buy much.

❛I never remember our milkman spilling a drop, even when the horse was a bit restive...❜

There were some advantages to receiving personal service in a smaller shop. People who lived alone or were very poor could ask for just an ounce or a pennyworth of goods, and those who found themselves hard up could 'strap' (run up a bill and pay when they had the money) if the grocer knew and trusted them.

▲ Shopping for vegetables hasn't changed much since the Twenties

▼ Co-operatives were groups of shops which bought in bulk to keep prices down, and paid out dividends – a share in the profits – to customers

Because there wasn't much money around in the Twenties, shopkeepers were constantly worried about going out of business. They had to work very hard indeed to win and keep their customers. This sometimes made life very difficult for the shopkeepers, but it was good from the customers' point of view, because they got such excellent service.

‘ You got wonderful service from the shops. And all the food shops always gave a family like ours (large and quite well-to-do) a present at Christmas. Atkinson's, the grocer's, would give one of their Christmas cakes in a lovely white box with silver writing on it and it always seemed very special, coming like that... ’

Small, less well-off families were wooed at Christmas too, but with presents more in keeping with the amount they spent.

‘ Every Christmas our grocer made us a gift of a rather nasty calendar and half a pound of inferior tea! ’

The following anecdote tells you quite a lot about the sort of personal, caring service some customers expected from their grocers – and got!

❛ As a child, I was once sent to a grocer's shop for a pound of butter. It was put in white greaseproof paper, then brown, then the string round. I was swinging this parcel, coming home, and it fell – right on to the muddy road! I dared not go home with it in that dirty condition. I took the brown paper off, and the string, and there was just this thin, white paper. I carried it home like that. I put it on the table and my mother said, 'Did they give it to you like that?' I just said, 'Yes.' And before I could say one word more, she was on the phone, ringing up the manager! He came round! You see, every customer mattered terribly. He said to me, 'You know very well I wrapped that parcel up properly for you, didn't I?'

I felt too ashamed to walk down the road afterwards . . . ❜

▲ Brown paper and string were used to wrap up the customers' purchases

# Pawn shops

▲ A pawn shop, with its sign of the three golden balls

Pawn shops are rare nowadays, but they did a flourishing trade in the Twenties. If you took an item into a pawn shop, the pawnbroker would lend you its value in ready cash. To redeem it, you had to return the money, plus a charge for the service.

Many poverty-stricken families could not have managed without the pawn, or 'pop' shop. It was a way of raising money to meet a crisis, or just a way to make ends meet from one week to the next.

You could pawn almost anything. Father's watch and chain was a popular item. So was his Sunday-best suit, because it wasn't needed for a whole week and could be redeemed when the pay-packet arrived on Friday, without any of the neighbours, or even Father himself, knowing it had gone.

❛ I've seen queues at the pawn shop on Monday mornings – husbands' suits going in. But there would be the hell to pay if they weren't out in time for church on Sunday! ❜

The very poor, who could never afford to redeem anything, were sometimes reduced to pawning essential items, like the mattresses, children's shoes and cooking utensils – until gradually there was nothing left and the family was totally destitute.

# Food

▲ A miner and his child having their tea

▲ A fish and chip shop

There were none of the pre-prepared foods that children like nowadays, such as fish-fingers and beef-burgers. There was no frozen food – nobody owned a deep-freeze – and tinned foods were very limited in content by modern standards. Instant coffee didn't come in until the early Thirties and foreign dishes like spaghetti, curry and risotto were unknown to most children. There were, however, fish and chips.

❛ No greaseproof paper or little trays with them in those days, you know – just newspaper with the print coming off on to the chips! ❜

Nobody ever asked children what they would like for a meal. Children in those days were expected to eat what they were given.

Middle class children ate fairly well.

❛ We had a cooked breakfast every morning and a substantial midday dinner, with steamed or milk pudding after meat and veg. But tea, even when I was twelve years old, was bread and jam and a slice of dry, home-made cake. Supper was a cup of cocoa and two plain biscuits. Towards the end of the Twenties, our income went up as food prices were going down. Then we had more fruit and cheese. With the new gas cookers, food was no longer liable to be half raw or burned. ❜

Butter on the bread at tea-time was a treat because it was very scarce and expensive after the War.

▲ Afternoon tea was a formal occasion for the middle and upper classes

Children from large, low-income families or children whose fathers were unemployed did not eat so well. Their parents couldn't afford to buy the foods that do you most good, such as meat, cheese, eggs and milk, or fresh vegetables. Often they weren't aware that one food was more nutritious than another. They filled the children up on cheaper foods like bread and margarine, jam, potatoes, tea and condensed milk, which didn't give them the necessary proteins and vitamins. As a result, large numbers of children grew up half-starved and fell prey to diseases like tuberculosis, rickets and anaemia, which attack badly nourished bodies.

Mothers of large families were notoriously under-nourished because they frequently did without food themselves for the sake of the children. Many mums existed on little more than 'cups of tea without milk and a slice of bread and margarine.'

❲ If we were friends of the vicar's daughter and went to church every Sunday, we got to be invited to the vicar's house to tea, which was always bread and butter with rhubarb and custard, one rock cake and a piece of toffee to go home with ... ❳

But new trends were on the way. By the late Twenties, American breakfast cereals such as cornflakes were gaining in popularity, and in 1929 sales of potato crisps reached a million packets a year.

One of the first advertisements for ▶ Kellogg's cornflakes

# At school

## Elementary schools

In the Twenties most children went to elementary school from the age of five up to the leaving age of fourteen. The elementary schools were free. Children who went to other schools (small private schools, preparatory, secondary or public schools) either won a scholarship or had families who could afford to pay the school fees.

Unfortunately, elementary schools were going through a difficult time and, as a result, many of the children suffered. The school buildings tended to be very out of date. Many had been built in Victorian times, for Victorian methods of teaching, with just one large room to accommodate several classes of children. Even by the mid-Twenties, many children were being taught in rooms which accommodated more than one class. Under those conditions, teaching had to be very strict and very formal. The first lesson of the day was scripture, followed almost entirely by the 3Rs (reading, writing and arithmetic).

By modern standards, schools had very little equipment.

'It was nearly all blackboard teaching. Very few text books were used and, except when writing compositions, we weren't encouraged to use our imaginations.'

'We were taught to read and do simple arithmetic, but no science and hardly any history or geography.'

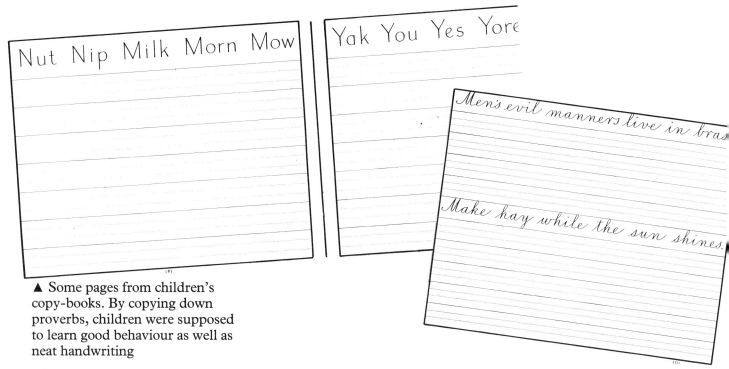

Nut Nip Milk Morn Mow

Yak You Yes Yore

Men's evil manners live in bras

Make hay while the sun shines.

▲ Some pages from children's copy-books. By copying down proverbs, children were supposed to learn good behaviour as well as neat handwriting

▼ More than one class was often taught in one room

▲ A secondary school classroom. Desks for older children had ink wells, and it was the job of the ink monitor to make sure these were kept full

In 1922 it was made compulsory for all children to stay on at school until they were at least fourteen. Before that, children who were over twelve years old had been allowed to leave school if they found a job, or to 'part-time', spend part of the day at work and part at school.

Difficulties arose because no proper provision was made for the extra numbers of older children who would be going to school. There was serious overcrowding, and not much thought had been given to what sort of lessons were appropriate for twelve to fourteen year olds. Sometimes they were given a partitioned-off corner of the schoolroom to themselves, but there were usually no rooms set aside where older children could go to receive instruction in a wider variety of subjects. Teachers often weren't trained to teach that age group and didn't know what to do with them. Many children were intensely bored. For clever children, the situation was often aggravated by the fact that they were allowed to jump standards (classes).

In the playground. In mixed schools, boys ▶ and girls had separate playgrounds and went into the school through separate entrances

❛ I arrived in the top class at twelve and so did two years there. I was just repeating and filling out time. I collected 'bank'. I took the headmaster's son's dinner on the bus to Victoria School, where he worked. (He wanted a hot meal and the headmaster's wife sent it in a basket for him). One day I was late and the bus conductress left the bus waiting while she came into the school to see if I was going! I decorated cushion covers with a stencil. Orders had been taken for them on Open Day, so I had to do them. I sat in with Class I or Class II if the teacher was absent . . . I was bored to death! ❜

▼ Westonbirt School, in Gloucester, opened in 1928

# Secondary schools

The only way in which a bright child could escape the boredom of the last years at the elementary school was by moving at the age of eleven to what was known as a secondary school.

A secondary school provided a wider range of subjects, such as Latin, French and science. But to get there, you had to have parents who could afford the fees, or you had to sit an exam to win a scholarship for a free place. Many clever children passed the exam but still couldn't go, even though the place was free. Their parents couldn't afford to buy the special uniform and extra items which these schools required. Often, parents needed their children to leave school and start earning wages as soon as they could.

A school report from a more progressive ▶ state school, which offered a wider variety of subjects than was usual

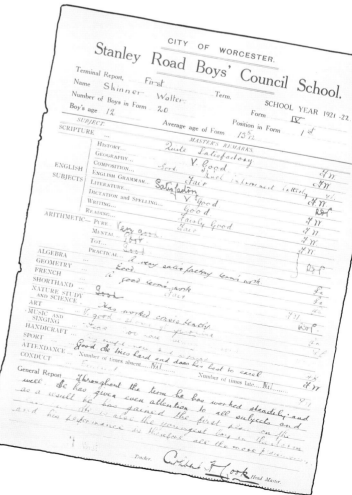

26

▲ Master and pupils at Harrow, one of the more famous boys' public schools. Only a very small minority of children went to these expensive schools

' There was some bitterness. I should, by merit and examination, have gone to a secondary school – I knew I never could because of the economic demands of my family. I had to go out to work for a living. At the same time, some of my classmates, better-off financially, but far less mentally, were proceeding to secondary school. This rankled in my mind for years . . . '

But life was not always easy for the children from working class homes who did manage to go to secondary school. It depended a lot on the school and the child. Some managed to fit in well, but many felt very out of place amongst all the middle class, fee-paying children.

' After passing a local free scholarship exam, I went to an exclusive High School for Girls for four years. I found it difficult to adjust to a life-style I hadn't realised existed. The pupils were daughters of medical consultants, lawyers, high-ranking churchmen, university dons and really wealthy local businessmen – while my father was an engineer earning about £4 a week! I also found it hard going to keep up with the high standard of learning expected of us. I found languages particularly difficult, as I was starting from scratch, whereas the other girls had at least two years learning behind them. None of my family could help me as they had only a very basic education.

Also, after moving to my new school, I rather lost touch with my old friends, and wouldn't have felt happy asking any of the new girls to my house. They would have found my family set-up quite astonishing and would have equated me with one of their housemaids. Those certainly weren't the happiest days of my life! '

# Uniform

Most children at fee-paying schools, and some at elementary schools, wore a uniform. For boys it was usually a flannel shirt and a grey serge suit. Short trousers were usually compulsory up to the age of fourteen, and all boys had to wear braces to hold up the trousers because they had baggy, unfitted waists.

' At my (boarding) school we had an everyday outfit of jacket and knee-length breeches. Once a week we wore our second-best outfit so that the everyday one could be cleaned and repaired. It was normally grey flannel in the week, dark suit on Sundays. '

▲ Short trousers were usually worn at school – even by older boys

◄ A gym-slip and white blouse was the most usual school uniform for girls

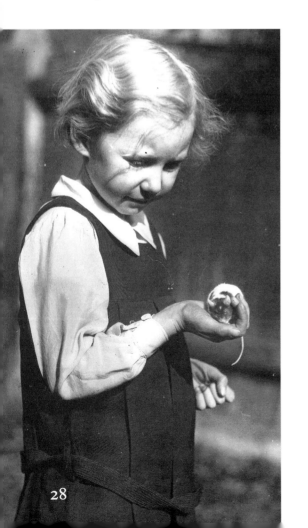

Both boys and girls wore the traditional cap, beret or boater and a tie in the school colours.

Girls usually wore a white blouse with a 'Peter Pan' collar, cardigan, gym-slip with box pleats (whose hem had to be precisely four inches above the knee), navy knickers, and black woollen stockings, which were much hated. There was a saying in the Twenties: 'What happens to girls in black stockings? Nothing!'

Summer uniform dresses were made with long sleeves. Boys from poorer families usually wore just short trousers and a jersey for school. Girls wore a skirt and knitted jumper, or a plain cotton dress in summer, which was 'very often your sister's, cut down'.

▲ Langley school, County Durham. Many country children walked several miles home for lunch and back each day

# Lunches

Elementary schools didn't provide pupils with lunch and, except in very rare cases, didn't have dining halls. Children went home for lunch if they could.

❛ I always walked home for lunch. It was about two miles each way so, in all, I walked eight miles a day to and from school, in all weathers. But eight miles wasn't unusual in those days . . . ❜

Children who couldn't get home for lunch ate their sandwiches in a classroom.

❛ As most of the children came such a long way and brought sandwiches for lunch, a large kettle was boiled on the schoolroom stove, and either the teacher or an older girl made Oxo or cocoa for their lunchtime drinks . . . ❜

But not all schools were so hospitable.

❛ At my school they ate in the cloakroom – hunks of bread and cheese, bread and jam, that sort of thing. They only ate in the classroom in really cold weather. They wouldn't have wanted to – they were always desperate to escape from the classroom! ❜

# Lavatories

Schools did provide lavatories, but usually they were outside. Many schools, especially those in the countryside, didn't have flush toilets. Pupils, and teachers too, had to cope with old-fashioned earth closets.

❛ The old earth closets at the back of the school where I taught were revolting – I couldn't face them! ❜

Even schools which did have flush lavatories didn't always provide wash-basins. 'Now wash your hands' was a rule they didn't bother too much about applying in those days.

❛ I can remember great excitement when water was finally laid on to three wash-basins. We had to teach the infants how to wash their hands . . . ❜

▼ A 'trough closet' or outside toilet at a school in London, 1929

# Discipline

Discipline was strict, whether you went to a free elementary school, or to a fee-paying school. Speaking in class, except to the teacher, was usually absolutely forbidden and could even get you the cane. Corporal punishment was given out for what would be considered quite minor offences today. Although, on the whole, pupils respected and liked their teachers, many felt that punishments were too severe at times.

' Punishment at our school for misbehaving included caning, rapping the knuckles with a ruler, lines, and being sent to Coventry. Most teachers were strict, but kind – though I remember one who was disliked by all the pupils in her class as she persistently pinched their arms and tugged their hair at the least provocation . . . '

' Every Wednesday morning we had to walk up the hill to church, and if we were late for church we had the cane! Often my mother sent me to the shop before school and I had to run like anything to get there on time . . . '

' In the junior school, you were stood in a corner until you got tired and asked to sit down. In the upper school, the cane was used quite a lot – for next to nothing, in fact! Being late, work not as good as it should be, talking in class . . . I think the whole set-up was completely wrong. '

' I was once reported by a prefect for eating chocolate on a station platform, and was sternly reprimanded by the headmistress for 'conduct unbecoming to a wearer of the school uniform'! '

▼ Teachers often sat raised up on high chairs so that they could keep an eye on the entire room

▲ A school netball team

# School Games

Many elementary schools had no Games fields and their pupils never got the chance of a proper Games lesson. It was different at the fee-paying public schools and secondary schools. At public schools in particular, being good at sport was more admired than being good at lessons.

❛ When we were cheering our school on at Games, I remember that if the juniors got excited, they dangled their hands from the wrists and shook them, saying, 'How ripping!' ❜

Boys played rugby, or sometimes had a choice of rugby or rowing in winter and cricket in summer.

❛ At Westminster, our uniform was morning coats and top hats; waistcoats, of course, and stiff collars. We went from Westminster to Putney to row, wearing all that lot! We rowed, got back into top hats, morning coats and striped trousers, and made our way home.

Through Putney High Street, Fulham, Camden Town. People shouting at you – insults! It was good training for life – carry any damn silly situation! ❜

Girls played hockey or lacrosse in winter and tennis in summer, though some tough-spirited girls' schools were starting to play cricket, too. Hard-playing girls were very much admired in the Twenties. The hockey team and lacrosse team were the 'bloods' (the fashionable 'in' set), as were the First XV and First XI in boys' schools.

❛ In our 'Dorothy bag' on the cloakroom peg, we had to keep a spare pair of black stockings, a pair of white plimsolls for PE and a black pair for Games – yes, plimsolls for hockey! So you can see why we needed a pair of dry stockings … ❜

Until the 1930s there were no teachers who were specially trained in either Games or PE, so all members of staff who were not too infirm were expected to lend a hand.

▲ These girls are exercising in the school playground by swinging short, weighted bars called dumb-bells

# Drill

Most schoolchildren in the Twenties, even at the better equipped schools, didn't have the benefit of a gym with special apparatus such as ropes and wallbars. Such things were for specialist gymnastics only.

PE usually took place in the playground or, if the weather was bad, in the school hall. It was known as 'drill' because a lot of the exercises were rather like army drill. Pupils were arranged in rows and, on sergeant major type commands from the teacher, they had to carry out a series of vigorous exercises.'

'Feet astride – place!
Hips – firm!
Trunk forward – bend!
Trunk forward – stretch!
Trunk upward – stretch!'

Drill wasn't so different from modern 'keep fit' and the aims were much the same: healthy bodies with correct posture, good physical co-ordination and mental concentration. Everybody was very fitness conscious in the Twenties, because there had been such a need for healthy fighting men in the War.

Pupils usually did drill in their ordinary school clothes. Boys had to remove detachable collars and tie their braces round their waists like belts. Under their school skirts, girls were supposed to wear sensible navy knickers which were not 'not too ample' and ended just above the knee. Suspenders for holding up stockings were thought more suitable for drill than garters, which cut off circulation.

A 'handkerchief drill' was recommended to start. It involved everybody producing a handkerchief and giving their nose a good blow, so that they could breathe really deeply. But, for obvious reasons, teachers usually seem to have missed it out!

# Jobs and pocket money

When part-time schooling was made illegal in 1922, children who were twelve or over were allowed to work for only two hours a day, one hour before morning school and an hour in the evening.

A lot of children worked, but not to earn themselves extra pocket money as they do today. Most did it because they belonged to a family which would have found it difficult to make ends meet without the extra cash the older children could bring in.

Paper rounds, milk rounds and delivering for shops were the most popular jobs.

‹ When I was twelve and a half years old, until I was fourteen, I helped at a local grocery store, weighing sugar and taking out orders at weekends, also serving in the shop after school hours. My wages were 3s.6d (18p) a week. I gave my mother 3s and had 6d for myself. There were six children in our family, so she was very glad of it. ›

‹ I did a milk round before school for a local dairy, on foot. It was not many calls, but I had to return each time with cans to be filled with the required order for each house. There were two of us boys. On one round the pay was 1s (5p) and on the other 1s.3d (6½p). ›

▼ Helping a painter and decorator

Because there were more very large families than there are today, and housework was so much harder without the help of labour-saving machines, many older girls were expected to help their mothers with the household chores, and with looking after their younger brothers and sisters.

❛ I always had to help with the washing on washday. We had a wash-house in the yard at the back, with a brick-built boiler and an old mangle which I had to keep turning. We always seemed to have an enormous amount of clothes to wash, and I had to make a large bucket of starch for the pillow-cases, pinafores, table cloths and covers . . . ❜

❛ My sister and I had to empty the potties from under the beds into a bucket and take it down three flights of stairs to the lavatory. We had to cut up newspapers into squares and tie them with string for lavatory paper. ❜

❛ As the eldest in a family of fourteen, I always had to take my brothers and sisters around with me. When I was asked by my friend to join the Band of Hope, Mum said I could only if I'd take some of the kids with me. So I turned up with five of them, and we all joined! ❜

Boys also helped. They dug the family allotment and did the heavier family chores.

▲ Collecting water for the family from an outside tap. Poor people often had to get all their water for washing, cooking and cleaning from one tap

◀ Dressed to help on the farm. The whole family were expected to help. Haymaking and harvest would often involve a whole village and be followed by a celebration

❛ My husband's sisters had to bath in the back bedroom. The brothers had to carry the hot water up, but after the bath, they poured it out over the sloping roof down to a drain hole at the back. ❜

But there were, of course, those fortunate ones who could claim:

❛ I never did any chores at all – never even made a bed. There were housemaids, kitchenmaids and so on . . . ❜

34

# Pocket money

On the whole, children did not expect to receive much pocket money. There weren't quite as many temptations to spend money as there are today, and the number of goods aimed especially at children was comparatively small. Sweets and comics were the main items.

❛ Every Friday my father gave us 3d (1½p) each and on bank holidays 6d (3p) each, with which we were quite pleased and happy . . ❜

❛ Money was tight. I had virtually no pocket money, but there was nothing to spend it on in term-time anyway. If ever I was given any money, as a present maybe, it was taken off me and put in the savings bank, or mother took charge of it. I never even saw it! I didn't handle money till after I left school, really . . . Nobody I knew discussed money. I had no idea what the old man earned, or any of the uncles. People didn't discuss incomes in those days. ❜

❛ When I was small we had 3d (1½p) a week, of which 1d went into the church collection and the other 2d into a money box to buy presents for others. This led to delinquency when we got a little older, in the sense that pennies for the Red Cross sometimes found their way into sweet shops . . . It was £1 a term in my teens. But 10s (50p) of that went on subs and things – Games fund, good causes etc. ❜

▲ The Boy's Own Paper was recommended by clergymen and headmasters as being 'healthy' reading for boys

But there were a few exceptions.

❛ There was one immensely rich boy at Westminster (School) who got half a crown (12½p) a working day! That was rich! ❜

35

# Clothes

In poorer and larger families, it was always a problem to provide footwear for the children.

' I remember all the children, girls as well as boys (in a country school) had enormous great lace-up boots on their feet. Button boots were too grand. There was no such thing as Wellingtons. They wore the same boots in summer. And in those days they didn't bother much about sizing... '

Girls were less encumbered by layers of petticoats and (older girls) by stiff, confining corsets than they had been before the War. But better-off children still wore plenty of underwear in winter. Before central heating, large family houses could be pretty draughty. There were 'scratchy wool vests, placed next to the skin', winceyette petticoats and garments called 'liberty bodices'.

By contrast, children from poor homes often didn't have any underwear at all.

' I never wore underpants, or a vest. I had no pyjamas: only a night shirt which was a shirt too shabby to wear in the daytime. Some neighbours had a big family and no money. They slept in muslin sacks with neck and armholes cut in because they couldn't afford nightwear. We used to see the sacks hanging out to dry on the washing line, and that's how we knew. There was no family allowance in those days to help buy clothes. '

▲ London shoppers – notice that they are all wearing hats

▼ Cloche hats, pulled well over the ears, were very popular

▲ In poorer families, children's clothes were often much mended hand-me-downs

▼ Sturdy lace-up boots were basic footwear for the poor, but the tabs to pull them on with were an extra – as were garters to hold up socks

For well brought up girls, hats and gloves were considered compulsory out-of-doors wear. Boys as well as girls commonly wore hats on the beach, and girls were expected to wear gloves in summer, even with long-sleeved dresses.

❛ Only when I went up to Cambridge (University) in 1936, were we daring enough to cycle around bare-headed. ❜

❛ I was once reported by a prefect because I had been seen in town without gloves on. ❜

37

▲ Drop-waisted dresses with irregular hems were the height of fashion

▼ Shiny black patent-leather shoes completed a fashionable outfit

Because school uniform was expensive, there was often not much money left to buy more exciting, casual clothes.

❛ I so badly wanted to have a pair of red or green court shoes, so fashionable around the mid-Twenties. But mine always had to be black Oxford shoes, suitable for school ... ❜

Children wore their old clothes to play in, usually something outgrown from the previous year.

❛ Other mothers inviting you out on a Saturday would say, 'Come in your dirt-clothes,' if you were going to play in the garden. In summer we wore home-made cotton dresses with knickers to match, so we could tuck our dresses into the knickers if we wanted to climb trees, because there were no jeans. ❜

Older boys and girls who had left school and managed to find a job enjoyed spending some of their money on the new fashions of the time. For girls especially, these were very exciting, simple and unencumbering, so different from the pre-war years!

❛ Most girls wore flesh-coloured lisle stockings and black patent shoes. Long strings of beads were all the rage, and dresses with low waistlines and a fringe at the hem. Also dresses made from cretonne curtain material, very chic we thought them! ❜

Hair was cut very short in styles called the 'bob', the 'shingle' and the 'Eton crop'. Many girls started to wear make-up, which shocked the mothers who had been brought up in Victorian and Edwardian times when make-up was thought very flighty.

❛ We would buy face powder from Woolworth's – 6d (2½p) a large box – 'California Poppy' or 'Evening in Paris' perfume for 1s (5p) and Pond's Cold Cream and Vanishing Cream for 6d a jar. We had our hair cut in the 'Eton crop' style for 6d. Incidentally, my mother would not allow me to use any make-up, and if I bought any she would take it away and put it on the fire, so I used to borrow my friend's make-up when we went to a dance and wash it off before I went home. ❜

Older boys wanting to cut a dash wore Oxford bags (flannel trousers with monstrously wide, floppy legs) and white silk, or artificial silk scarves.

❛ I remember a senior boy who came back one term with a pair of Oxford bags, though they were not allowed in term time. He was a 'blood', so he got away with it. I'd probably have had them taken off me by a few bullying hands . . . ❜

▲ From an advertisement for 'Start-rite' shoes. Prices for these shoes ranged from about 5s (25p) for children's shoes, to 27s (£1.35) for adult shoes

# Entertainment

## The pictures

Going to the pictures became the favourite evening entertainment for almost everyone in the Twenties. In large towns there would be several cinemas, all showing different films, and all would be changing their films twice a week. With such a lot of choice, and no competition from television, people sometimes went to see two or three films a week.

Moving pictures weren't new. They dated from before the First World War, but their quality had vastly improved. Short, jerky films were replaced with lengthier ones which told stories. They were still silent, and in black and white, but many were brilliantly made. The scenes they showed and the stunts they used were brand-new and very exciting to audiences then.

Charlie Chaplin and Harold Lloyd films were considered good family viewing.

❛ We were only supposed to see selected films. 'Robin Hood' with Douglas Fairbanks Senior was thought okay for children . . . and Charlie Chaplin was allowed. But sometimes I slipped off in the hols with my brother to see a wildwest . . . ❜

Stars of romances, such as Ramon Navarro and Rudolph Valentino became the idols of millions of young girls, like the pop stars of today.

◀ Charlie Chaplin's many films included 'The Kid', in 1921, and 'The Gold Rush', in 1925

Rudolph ▶ Valentino starred in romantic silent films, such as 'The Son of the Sheik', made in 1921

'Most girls found Rudolph Valentino and Ramon Navarro very exciting and maybe in a rather gentle way they made us aware of sensual feelings. But we often found the courting couples in the back row more interesting than the film!'

'The adolescent girl's fantasy at that time was the White Slave Trade! We fantasised about getting snatched and bundled into a taxi on the way to school...'

The early picture houses were often converted from old buildings, such as chapels or schools. They didn't always aim to provide comfort.

'When my friend and I were on day-shift together, we would go to the cinema for 3d (1½p), sitting in what were known locally as the 'horse boxes' – wooden seats with a strip of carpet tacked on, almost like church pews.'

Cinema organs were able to create all kinds of ▶ different sounds to accompany a film

▼ A public hall, converted into a cinema to satisfy the sudden demand

But by the mid-Twenties, sumptuous new buildings – 'picture palaces' – were being built. Their interiors were decorated in the 'height of luxury and good taste', with comfortably upholstered tip-up seats, elegant foyers, balconies and balcony-level cafes – all aimed at attracting middle class audiences.

Small, local cinemas had to make do with a pianist, or a trio consisting of piano, drums and violin, to give a musical accompaniment to the film. But the larger, more splendid 'picture palaces' had giant electric organs which attracted audiences from miles around.

41

◄ Many cinemas had hard wooden chairs, not the plush seats we have in cinemas today

Because so many homes were still without washing facilities, all picture houses were seen as breeding grounds for germs and bugs. Local picture houses attracted the nickname 'flea-pits', which has stuck to the present day. In the intervals an usherette might come round with a pump-up spray can of disinfectant, shallowly disguised with an overlay of perfume (a smell remembered with great nostalgia) which she puffed between the aisles to freshen the atmosphere, and deaden the smell of oranges and monkey nuts, which were popular with 1920s audiences.

Despite many technical improvements, a film did not always run smoothly, especially in the early part of the decade. Breakdowns were frequent and got a riotous reception from audiences who had not forgotten the 'join in and jeer' atmosphere of the old music halls and travelling theatres.

❛ We stamped and raved and whistled until the film was renewed or a second reel put on. The manager used to appear and appeal for order, and we were asked to listen to a musician – a valiant pianist, struggling against the odds. At the Grand, more often than not, when the second reel was put on or the film restarted, it would be upside down because the operator was a confirmed drunkard who would start the film, then adjourn to a nearby pub for a pint or two, returning only when he thought it was time to change the reel. ❜

▲ Usherette at The Carlton Cinema, Upton Park, which was opened in 1928

A 'chucker-out' would be on hand to deal with the more rowdy elements.

Many purpose-built cinemas also included a stage and dressing rooms for music hall style variety acts, just in case the popularity of films should suddenly fade.

❮ The Grand was not only a cinema, but on occasions would stage a 'Grand Review' consisting of a comic, baritone and soprano and six chorus girls. On these occasions an extra charge was made. At Christmas and the New Year, the same party would produce a 'Grand Pantomime'. ❯

In 1928 the announcement 'See and hear Al Jolson in "The Jazz Singer"; A Singing and Talking Film' led to great changes. The 'talkies' had arrived! Cinema proprietors rushed to get their houses wired for sound and, overnight, many excellent musicians found themselves out of work. In the presence of stars who talked, audiences became quieter and more docile.

▲ One of the new 'flea-pits', built quickly and cheaply

▼ The Capitol, one of the grander, purpose-built cinemas

# The wireless

❝ We had one of the first wirelesses in the village, because I made it myself when I was about fourteen... ❞

In 1920, wireless was known to most people in Britain only as a means of sending messages to ships at sea. But in November 1922, the British Broadcasting Company began to make regular broadcasts. Wireless became an exciting new form of entertainment.

The crystal set, a type of wireless which could be made at home, was very popular because it cost much less than those sold in the shops. It cost 15s (75p) or less, as opposed to £25 for a ready-made set with only two valves. Both types needed earphones, and everybody else in the house had to keep very quiet because the signal was so weak. Many crystal sets were made for the family by schoolboys who were quick to pick up the new scientific know-how and vocabulary. Building sets became quite a craze, as much for the fascination of constructing and fiddling with them, as for actually listening in.

By the end of the decade, wireless sets had become more compact. Loudspeakers had improved so much that headphones were no longer essential. People were able to listen to the wireless while moving around and doing other things.

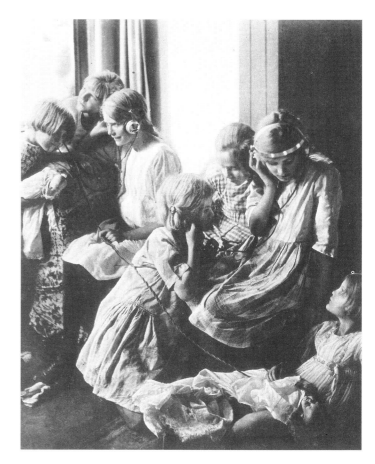

▲ Taken in 1923 for a photographic exhibition, this photograph was entitled 'Children's Hour' and shows children using earphones to listen to the radio

▼ The Radio Times was first published 28 September 1923

▲ A 'palais de danse' in East London

# Dancing

Dancing was all the rage, not only with the rich 'bright young things' at private parties and clubs, but with older boys and girls from all classes. They flocked to public dance halls (often given the title 'palais de danse') or to local dances held at the school or village hall, or at the tennis club. They danced to jazz bands and indulged in all the lively dance sensations from the USA.

❛ At the Sixpenny Hop, as we called the Friday night dance, we would dance the Charleston and Black Bottom, with the band accompanied by saxophonists and trumpets playing all the popular songs like 'Me and Jane in a Plane', 'Brown Eyes, Why Are You Blue?', 'Vo-do-de-oh-do' and so on. Soft drinks only were served and the boys were courteous to the girls, asking if they might have the pleasure of this dance ... But boy-friends were not encouraged by my parents and I had to be home by ten o'clock. ❜

Parents were usually very strict about staying out late.

❛ You got into trouble for staying out late. Most parents were very strict about that. Even in my late teens, I had to be in by nine o'clock sharp. If I was one minute late, my father would be waiting at the gate to know where I'd been. ❜

There was often a shortage of young men at dances because an appalling number had been killed in the Great War. As a result, girls took to dancing with each other, and the sight of two girls dancing together became socially acceptable.

❛ We went to dance halls a lot when I was about sixteen. Groups of us girls would go and dance together. Boys? Oh, we didn't care if they asked us or not ... ❜

# Pastimes and hobbies

Picnicking and long country walks were popular pastimes, especially for those with not much money to spare for entertainment. Sunday afternoon was a time when the whole family might set out for a long walk.

❛ When I was a child we went out for walks as a family. We walked into the country, picked wild flowers, had lemonade and twopenny packets of biscuits at a pub and sometimes came home on the tram ... ❜

Snakes and ladders, ludo and chess were popular indoor games, and crossword puzzles were introduced from the USA.

Other pastimes for wet afternoons were playing the piano, listening to the gramophone, dressing up and putting on shows, or playing shops.

There were plenty of good children's books to read, and comics and magazines, such as The Magnet, The Boy's Own Paper and The Girl's Own Paper. There was also the Children's Newspaper, which covered all the major news items in a simple style, though it wasn't popular with all children.

❛ Being an avid reader, my mother thought the Children's Newspaper would interest me, and had it delivered every week. But I found it very boring and preferred to escape to the lavatory and read 'The News Of The World'! ❜

▲ A picnic in the country. People were no longer shocked by the sight of women smoking cigarettes in public, and these two are even smoking cigars

▼ Skipping games in the street – in those days, cars were not such a danger to children playing

Making collections was popular. One craze was for collecting cards out of cigarette packets. Lots of men had started smoking during the War. Now many women took it up. You could either stick your cigarette cards in an album or use them for a game called 'skimming'. There were several versions of skimming. You could try to skim your card so that it landed on top of your opponent's, you could skim the cards at a wall, seeing who could get their cards nearest to it, or you could line some cards up against the wall and skim other cards at them to see who could knock most over.

In the Twenties, there was much less traffic than there is today and it was safer for children to play in the street.

❛ When we had skipping games, the rope would be stretched right across the street. We would skip to jingles (like 'Salt! Mustard! Vinegar! Pepper!') and do bumps. All the children lined up for their turn. ❜

❛ Boys played marbles along the gutters, which it would be too dangerous to do now. They jumped off walls with clothes props – which sometimes broke! ❜

In the dark winter months, groups of children used to congregate in the pools of light cast by the gas lamps. They played a noisy game called kick-can. It was a bit like hide-and-seek, except that the person who was 'it' had to chase after a tin can which one of the group kicked as far as he could. Sometimes they got into a bit of mischief.

❛ We played 'knocking down ginger'. You tied a string to two door knockers, pulled on it and ran away . . . ❜

# Out and about

All the old, pre-war forms of transport were still in use in the early Twenties. If you wanted to get from one part of town to another, you took an electric tram which ran on tracks down the middle of the road. If you were fortunate enough to make a long journey, you took a steam train. Horses were still used quite a lot. Tradesmen delivered their goods to your door by horse and cart, and horses were still used for transporting heavy loads along the roads. Loads too heavy for horses were hauled by steam locomotives.

▲ Electric trams could move large numbers of passengers more quickly and easily than the first motor-buses. But they ran along tracks which were set into the road, and these sometimes interfered with other vehicles

❛ The baker, milkman, greengrocer and coalman all called at the door with horse-drawn carts. Keen gardeners kept watch, and if the horse left a deposit, someone was out in a flash with shovel and bucket. No sense in wasting good manure! ❜

▼ Horse-drawn carts were still used for deliveries

▼ A humorous postcard from Wensleydale entitled, 'A car on the road is worth two in the ditch'

NSLEYDALE—"A CAR ON THE ROAD IS WORTH

For lots of people, especially the young, the bicycle was their chief means of getting around. Outside the cities, roads were far safer for bicycle riders than they are today.

But throughout the Twenties, changes were steadily taking place. Trams gradually began to be replaced by trolley-buses or motor-buses, and motor-lorries took over the heavy transport. The motorcycle and, above all, the motor car became increasingly popular methods of private transport.

Just after the First World War, a motor car was a great luxury which only the rich could afford. But methods of mass production brought the costs down until, by about 1925, a small car came within the reach of the middle classes. An average priced family vehicle was around £300. But that was still more than a skilled workman earned in a year, so if your family owned a car you were considered well-off. It was a great status symbol and often used only on special occasions.

Throughout the decade, the cost of a car actually went down! By 1929 you could buy a Morris Cowley for £195. Cars had become more common everyday things.

‘ In the mid-Twenties, I can remember only about three cars in the whole village: a Model T Ford owned by the carpenter, which was used as a taxi; the doctor had one; and a rich farmer. The miller had a motorbike, and he was involved in the first accident I can remember. ’

The question of whether women should be allowed to drive began to create quite a lot of controversy, but nevertheless an increasing number of women took over the wheel.

‘ We were fortunate enough to have a car in the early Twenties, a bull-nose Morris. Father refused to drive over the twenty miles an hour speed limit, though everybody else did – Mother wasn't so cautious, so she took over . . . ’

▼ A steam train

# Learning to drive

Motorcycles, and motorcycles with sidecars attached, were cheaper than cars, so before the mid-Twenties they outnumbered cars on the roads. Motorcycles were most frequently driven by show-off young men at a rather fast speed with their girlfriends riding pillion (side-saddle, and even, occasionally, two at a time, since there was no law governing how many went on a bike).

Throughout the decade you could buy a driving licence at sixteen, and one for a motorcycle at fourteen. There were no tests for learners and no driving schools either! You learned from a friend or relative, or sometimes from the car salesman.

‘In those days, if you bought a car, the firm you bought it from would often teach you to drive for nothing. You could take as long as you liked. Driving was very different. There was no such thing as yellow lines, and not half the regulations. If you wanted to visit a shop, you pulled up in front of it. You stayed as long as you wanted. And if it was a grocer's, they always used to carry your stuff out and put it in for you. ’

▲ A motorcycle and sidecar could take a small family: father on the bike and mother and children in the sidecar

▲ The Strand, London, 1922. Horse-drawn carriages were still a fairly common sight. At the beginning of the Twenties, motor cars were a luxury for the rich

With the increased number of motor vehicles on the roads, the number of accidents inevitably rose, especially in cities, and caused a lot of anxiety. The law governing motoring was way behind the times. It had not been changed since 1903! The problem was debated in the House of Commons in 1924. Lord Lamington, who started the debate, said,

‘ You are walking along and see nothing in the shape of a motor vehicle. And then all at once you hear the swish of one of these juggernauts rushing along at a speed far in excess of twenty miles an hour. You are almost overwhelmed by it before you realize that there is any vehicle anywhere in your neighbourhood. It is not fair that these frightful risks should be incurred by the general public. ’

▲ Heavy traffic on Oxford Street, London – notice there are no street signs or traffic lights

▼ Policemen were needed to direct the traffic

Hand signals were introduced and more policemen were put on duty at major road intersections. But traffic lights were not experimented with until 1929, and the 1903 law on motoring was not updated until 1930.

# Holidays

‘ Our holidays were very modest affairs. A few days by the sea at a near-by resort, in our case along the Bristol Channel. Just in rooms, never an hotel . . . ’

Families who could afford a holiday usually headed for a week by the sea in a British boarding-house. Resorts such as Blackpool, whose famous 'illuminations' were drawing crowds even then, became increasingly popular throughout the Twenties.

Some people were encouraged to take continental holidays because, after the War, prices on the continent were much cheaper than in Britain. But compared with today very few people went abroad on holiday.

Most people couldn't afford to go on holiday at all.

‘ We never had a holiday when I was young. We couldn't afford it. My honeymoon in Bournemouth was the first . . . ’

As well as paying for travel and accommodation, they had to budget for a loss of earnings, because paid holidays were not common until the late 1930s. Workers could not usually afford to take more than a day or two off, even if they spent it at home.

▲ Donkey rides were a popular part of the British seaside holiday

On the steps of a boarding-house, Cleethorpes. In the ▼ early Twenties, it was still common for holiday-makers in a boarding-house to buy their own food, which would be cooked for them by their landlady

◄ Bathers pose for a holiday photograph at a crowded swimming-pool in Blackpool

▲ A charabanc outing. The first charabancs were open wagons pulled by horses. Early motor-coaches, like this one, were also called charabancs

▼ Organised seaside entertainment for children

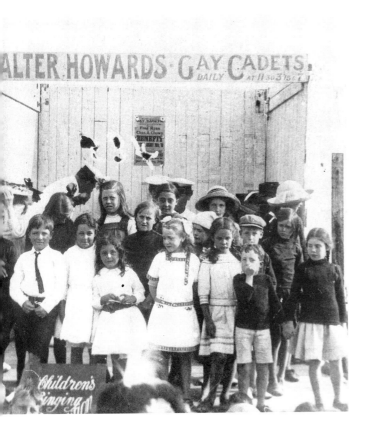

❛ My father took me to London to visit the Empire Exhibition at Wembley, and that one hundred and twenty miles was the longest journey I made until I was twenty years old. ❜

For most people, a journey of a hundred miles would have been a very special and memorable experience. In 1924 the big exhibition held at Wembley, in celebration of the British Empire, tempted many to make their longest-ever journey from home. A lot of children visited the exhibition on rail excursions with the schools.

Some young people who belonged to the Scouts or Guides had the opportunity to go to camp. Many others got away only for a bank holiday day trip in a vehicle called a charabanc. Day trips were often organised by the local Sunday school, factory or pub. People would put a small amount of money aside each week until they had saved enough for the trip. Sometimes a whole street organised an outing. They usually went to the nearest seaside resort or beauty spot. 'And you paid in all year for it!'

# Sport

Professional sport started to draw huge crowds of supporters. Working people who now had more free time, and thousands who were unemployed, took advantage of the easier methods of transport to flock to sports grounds and stadiums.

Football became the great favourite. But the atmosphere at matches was very different from today.

 ❛ My father used to give me 5d (2½p) on a Saturday dinner time. 4d admission and 1d for sweets. It was a real treat to watch, and *no violence*, no matter who won or lost. ❜

International matches hardly attracted any support and there were no enormous transfer fees.

In 1923 Wembley Stadium was opened. The first Cup Final to be played there was between Bolton Wanderers and West Ham. Bolton won, 2–0. The match attracted such enormous crowds that they broke down the barriers and overflowed on to the pitch. But in those days that was a very unusual occurrence.

▲ Supporters at a football match between Arsenal and Newcastle, 1923 – almost everyone is wearing a cap

▼ A huge crowd packed Wembley Stadium for the first Cup Final. Before the match started, supporters rushed on to the pitch. Many who were refused entry scrambled over the barriers to get into the grounds

Cricket enjoyed immense popularity too, especially with the middle classes. Racecourses and greyhound tracks drew large crowds who gambled heavily.

Tennis was winning more enthusiasts, both to watch and to play. Women particularly admired the style of the professionals on the new Centre Court at Wimbledon. A French star, Suzanne Lenglen, was hero-worshipped by British crowds in the first half of the Twenties. She set the fashion for wearing special tennis clothes.

To achieve more freedom of movement, she introduced the idea of a simple, short pleated skirt and a short-sleeved top. Before that, women had played in their ordinary summer dresses. Women players continued to wear stockings. Not until the Thirties did they ever appear on the tennis court bare-legged.

Ice-skating enjoyed a brief fashion. Many cities built skating-rinks, but most have since disappeared. Public swimming-baths were also an attraction to those who could afford the admission.

▼ Queen Mary congratulates Suzanne Lenglen at Wimbledon. Mademoiselle Lenglen was the women's singles champion at Wimbledon from 1919 to 1923 and again in 1925

▼ Tennis wear for women became less restrictive, but stockings were still considered essential

# Illness

‹ In 1922, when I was eight years old, I went down with diphtheria and spent Christmas in Newtown Isolation Hospital. I was in there, ill, for three months. Then my mother signed a form to have me home. My sisters had to go and stay in friends' homes while I was kept in the bedroom for another few weeks. Then the house was fumigated. ›

In the Twenties there was no vaccination against any of the contagious diseases, apart from smallpox. Outbreaks of whooping-cough, scarlet fever, diphtheria and measles spread like wildfire, especially in the poorer overcrowded city areas, where they were helped by malnutrition and poor sanitation. All these diseases could be killers, but the greatest scourge of all was tuberculosis; in the early Twenties it claimed almost as many victims as all the other diseases put together.

Throughout the decade, as living conditions gradually improved, the number of deaths from contagious diseases decreased. But even if you survived a serious illness, you still ran the risk of complications, such as broncho-pneumonia which could damage your lungs or even kill you. In those days, measles often resulted in permanent deafness or poor eyesight.

When youth meets youth

It's sturdy health that wins
—and Lifebuoy helps

What a struggle! Sometimes you're on the right side of the line, sometimes slipping over. Like life itself! Like the fight for health!

Get Lifebuoy to pull behind you. Personal cleanliness is more than half the battle, all doctors agree. Put your faith in Lifebuoy Soap, for in it there is a wonderful health element which penetrates deep down into the pores of the skin, driving out all impurities. That is why wise mothers teach their families the Lifebuoy habit—and keep the germs at bay.

# Lifebuoy Soap
## FOR HEALTH

LEVER BROTHERS LIMITED, PORT SUNLIGHT

◄ People were becoming more aware of the importance of hygiene

▼ Severe malnutrition was not uncommon in children. Fortunately, with proper care and a nutritious diet, this child recovered

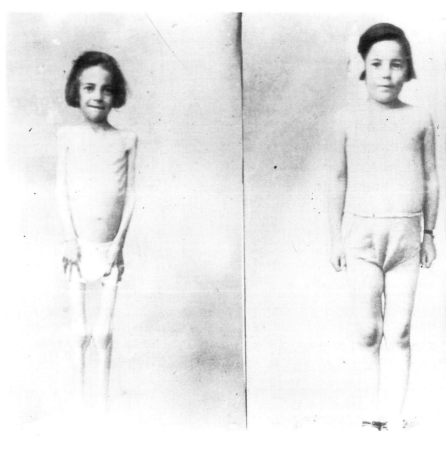

56

# Why catch their Influenza?

**Y**OU need not! Just carry Formamint with you and suck these delicious tablets whenever you are in danger of being infected by other people.

"Suck at least four or five a day"—so says Dr. Hopkirk in his standard work "Influenza"—for "in Formamint we possess the best means of preventing the infective processes which, if neglected, may lead to serious complications."

Seeing that such complications often lead to Pneumonia, Bronchitis, and other dangerous diseases, it is surely worth while to protect yourself by this safe, certain, and inexpensive means. Protect the children, too, for their delicate little organisms are very exposed to germ-attack, especially during school-epidemics. Be careful, however, not to confuse Formamint with so-called formalin tablets, but see that it bears the name of the sole manufacturers: Genatosan, Limited (British Purchasers of Sanatogen Co.), 12, Chenies Street, London, W.C. 1. (Chairman: The Viscountess Rhondda.)

*"Attack the germs before they attack you!"*

Though genuine Formamint is scarce your chemist can still obtain it for you at the pre-war price — 2/2 per bottle. Order it to-day.

# *Formamint*
## THE GERM KILLING THROAT TABLET

▲ Patent medicines from the chemist were often cheaper than a visit to the doctor

▼ Rules for sickness and quarantine, from Mrs Beeton's Household Management, 1921 edition

Without antibiotics, all sorts of other illnesses and minor infections, such as ear infections, lasted longer and led to complications likely to damage your health. It's hardly surprising that people were fussier about what we think of as the milder diseases, such as chicken pox, German measles and mumps. The idea of inviting your friends round to catch it and 'get it over with' wasn't unknown, but it was firmly discouraged.

| Disease | When the patient ceases to be infectious | Quarantine required after latest exposure to infection |
|---|---|---|
| Chicken pox | When every scab has fallen off | 20 days |
| Diphtheria | About 4 weeks after commencement, if no complications | 12 days |
| German measles | 10 days after appearance of rash | 20 days |
| Measles | 2 weeks after appearance of rash | 16 days |
| Mumps | 3 weeks | 24 days |
| Scarlet fever | 6 weeks, or when sore throat albuminuria and desquamation have disappeared | 10 days |
| Smallpox | When every scab has fallen off | 16 days |
| Typhus fever | 4 weeks | 14 days |
| Whooping-cough | 5 weeks, or 2 weeks after cough and whooping have disappeared | 21 days |

# School medical inspections

Inspections in poorer areas revealed many cases of tuberculosis and rickets (a disease which deformed your bones and was caused by malnutrition). There were also plenty of minor diseases and irritations, such as nits, ringworm, and a skin disease called impetigo, from which even teachers were not immune.

❝ I suffered from sores on my face for several years, which I believe was impetigo picked up from the children. ❞

▲ After 1907, regular medical inspections were made compulsory in schools

# Paying the doctor

❝ My father was always ill because of rheumatism. We paid a doctor's collector every week, but we were always in debt. We never caught up. The doctor's bills were put on a spike. Every time you paid 6d (2½p) you got a receipt and that was put on another spike. Every so often we checked one pile against the other to see how much we were in debt. ❞

There was no National Health Service in the 1920s. There were insurance schemes, but they usually only covered the wage earner and not the rest of his family. In any case, not every worker had insurance. If you were ill and not covered by insurance, you had to pay the doctor for his services. Many poorer families paid a small sum to the doctor's collector each week: '6d, or as much as you could afford'. By doing that, a small and normally healthy family could just about pay the doctor's bills. But if a member of the family was often ill, or several fell ill at once, it was very easy to get into debt.

Usually, poorer families went to a doctor only when the illness became serious. Minor ailments weren't treated at all: people 'put up' with them. Poor eyesight and bad teeth frequently went untreated because opticians' and dentists' services weren't usually covered by insurance schemes. A genuine fear of the dentist held some people back. Visiting the dentist was an unknown and therefore terrifying experience.

❝ If your teeth were all bad, you could have the lot taken out for nothing at the Infirmary. But you had nothing to replace them – you wouldn't be able to afford a set of false teeth! ❞

◀ A spoon of malt a day was said to keep the doctor away

**Don't give in**
until you have tried
VIROL-and-MILK

Many a woman, looking in the mirror, is distressed to see the little worried lines which write the story of nerve-fag between her brows and about the corners of her mouth. She feels she is getting to look ill-tempered and older than her age. She puts it down to over-work, anxiety, need of change, perhaps, or need of repose —but the underlying cause is under-nourishment of the nervous tissues. She ought to take Virol and Milk.

Milk—Nature's most sustaining of foods, and Virol – with its world famous restorative and tissue-building qualities – are here combined in a new form to produce a beverage unrivalled for soothing and re-energising an overtaxed nervous system. The worried feeling and the worried look depart when Virol and Milk is regularly taken, and in their place come a serene, cheerful energy, abundantly able to cope with the daily irritations of a strenuous life. You will not find your work "too much for you" if you take Virol and Milk.

Virol and Milk is delicious in flavour, more nourishing and more digestible than milk alone. Make yourself a cup in the middle of the morning and last thing at night—it only takes a minute—and it will do you "a world of good."

**VIROL**
AND
**MILK**
IN GOLDEN POWDER

Prepared in a Moment

In Tins 4/3 and 2/6
(Trial size, 1/6).
The new 4/3 size contains twice as much as the 2/6 size.

Virol Ltd., Hanger Lane, Ealing, London, W.5.

"Simply add Hot Water"

# Self-help

People tried to avoid the crippling cost of medical treatment by trying out home cures or buying patent medicines from the chemist.

❛ My only childhood ailment was measles. No doubt my healthy body was due to my daily dose of 'Virol', and my healthy bowels due to taking 'California Syrup of figs' every Friday night. ❜

❛ In spring, mother gave us sulphur in little cone packets. She blew it into our mouths from the narrow end so that it went down our throats to keep them free from illness. A mixture of vinegar and butter was good for sore throats. You put it into the oven to make it hot – it made you gulp when you went to drink it. There was brimstone and treacle by the spoonful for coughs. Cod liver oil was horrible! ❜

❛ Each year in spring, my father went to a local brewery with a two pound jam jar. This was filled with 'barm', which was yeast working on top of the vat. It was kept outside on the window-sill of the kitchen, and each morning we had to have a teaspoonful before school. ❜

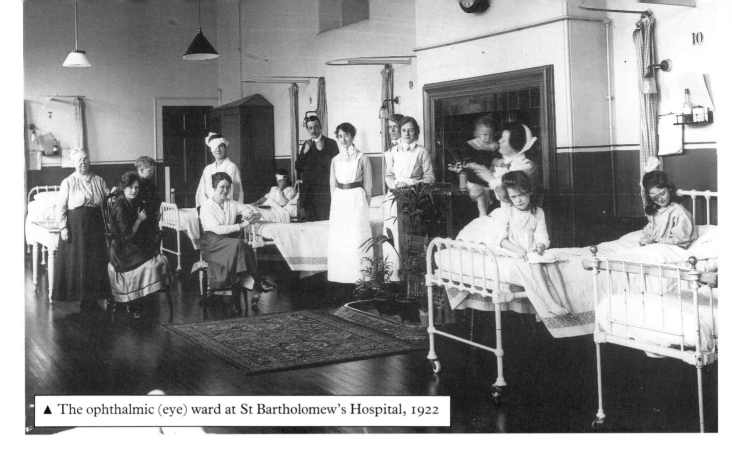

▲ The ophthalmic (eye) ward at St Bartholomew's Hospital, 1922

People also helped each other.

‘ We were more neighbourly then – we had to be if we'd no money! I can remember my mother turning out often to help. ’

In the Twenties many women had their babies without the expensive assistance of a doctor or a trained midwife. There was usually a woman in the neighbourhood who had experience helping with childbirth, and she would visit for only a shilling or two. There were other women who could be sent for to sit with the sick, or 'lay out' bodies.

Many women began to learn how to limit the number of children they had. But people didn't talk much about the facts of life. Until well into their teens, a lot of children were ignorant of how babies are made and how they are born.

‘ My parents never told me the facts of life. I found out about it from older children. I was about sixteen before I really knew where babies came from. Until then, I thought your stomach split open! ’

# In hospital

Conditions in hospitals were poor compared with today. Many hospitals had no special children's wards and visiting, even by parents, was often limited to twice a week.

Hospital beds had to be paid for, unless they were covered by special insurance contributions. There were a few free beds for the very poor, which could be obtained with the help of a note from the local vicar or a wealthy benefactor of the hospital. The only alternative was treatment at the out-patients or the workhouse. The workhouse was a place for paupers with no home and no money, so that was a desperate last resort.

Cases which would nowadays only be dealt with in hospital were frequently dealt with at home; even when minor surgery was involved.

‘ I had my infected tonsils removed lying on the kitchen table at home, by our own GP, assisted by his partner as anaesthetist. A neighbour who chanced to look through the window while this was going on, promptly keeled over with shock! ’

▲ A picnic in Epping Forest
Cooling off in the river ▶

# Fears

❝ As a child, you could just go straight out and run across the road into the fields and knew you'd be safe. There didn't seem to be the wickedness there is now . . . ❞

Crime was something most people associated only with large towns and cities. On the whole, children didn't have the same fear of murderers, muggers or child-molesters as children today. Theft was the most common crime, but few thefts involved violence.

There were even fewer murders than before the War, and the chances of getting murdered by a stranger were remote. In 1928, London was said to be the safest capital city in the world.

❝ You never heard about people getting mugged or beaten up in those days. We didn't have much money, but I think we were more honest . . . ❞

❝ I used to take my little brothers and sisters off for the day picnicking, and everywhere seemed safe – no traffic on the country roads and no child-molesters in the woods . . . ❞

If there was anything horrific in the newspaper, like a report of a murder, most parents made sure that their children did not read about it.

❝ The newspaper was kept strictly away from us. When we were fourteen or fifteen, we still weren't allowed to read about things like that. Nor were any of our friends . . . ❞

Children looked up to people in authority, such as policemen and teachers, more than they do today. Everybody knew the local 'bobby', and he did not hesitate to hand out punishment on the spot for minor offences.

‘ Our local policeman was called PC Brotherton. We were scared to death of him! If he caught you scrumping, it was a clout round the ear! ’

Fathers didn't often talk about their experiences in the trenches, but the sight of blind or mutilated ex-servicemen in the street brought home to children some of the horrors of war.

‘ Living in Brighton, we often saw the blind ex-servicemen from St Dunstan's. No one had sun glasses in the early Twenties, so when we saw these men with their small, round black lenses, we thought they had black holes instead of eyes! Dolls in those days had moveable eyes which used to 'fall in'. Thinking of the blind men, my sister used to scream with fear when that happened. ’

◀ A policewoman sorts out some mischief

Many of the fears which children had then were just the same as those which children have today, such as getting into trouble with parents or teachers, being left out, or being bullied by other children at school.

‘ One occasion I recall concerned half a dozen of the oldest lads. They developed a stunt whereby one lad was held head downwards down the toilet while somebody flushed it. On being found out, the headmaster was absolutely furious with them and they were all caned in turn. ’

Ironically, what people in the Twenties had no fear of at all was the possibility of another war. Nobody then suspected that World War II lay not so very far round the corner. 'We thought we'd just fought the War to end Wars!'

' Children today seem to have so much freedom in comparison to us. They do so many different things. But we had a happy time, despite everything. People seemed able to trust each other. But now, you don't feel safe to go out by yourself at night. It wasn't just because we were living in a village – it was general. I know we've gained a lot since the Twenties, but we've also lost a lot. To my mind, something important's gone out of life since then . . . Do you understand what I mean . . . ? '

◄ Many people think of the Twenties as a time of new fashions, parties and having fun. But for people who were unemployed or on low wages, there were real fears of hunger, illness and homelessness

# Index

The page numbers shown in **dark letters** refer to illustrations.